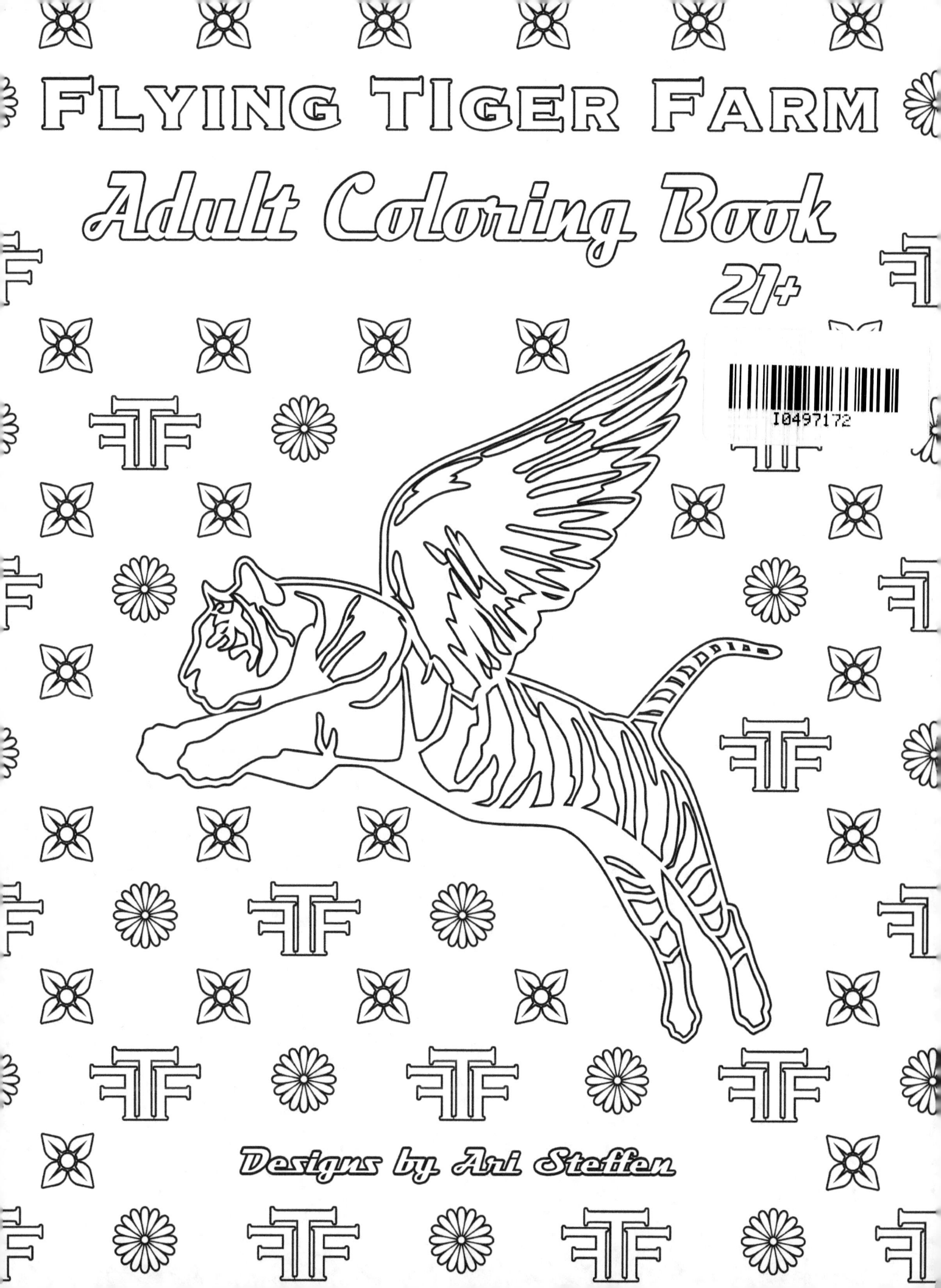

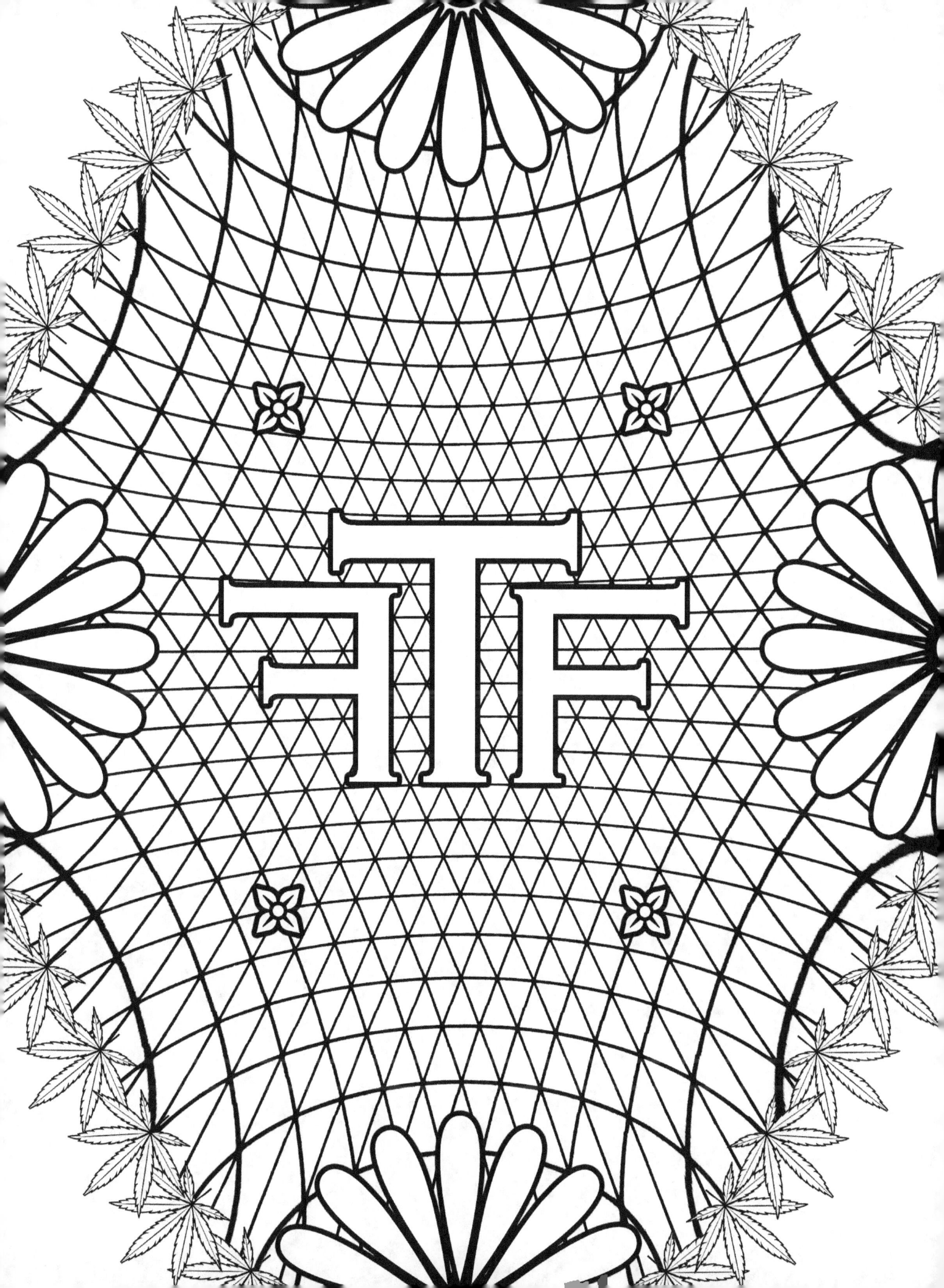

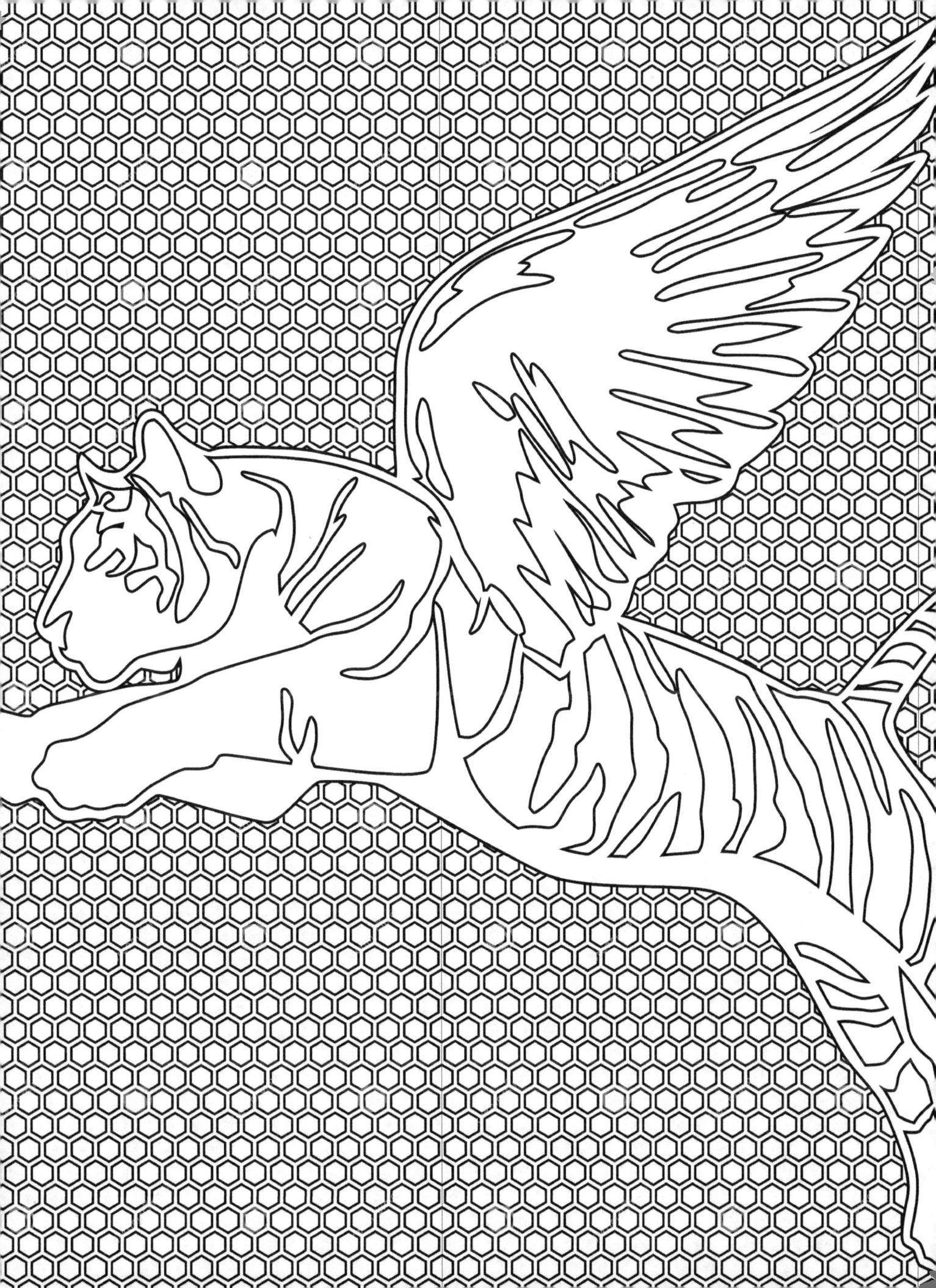

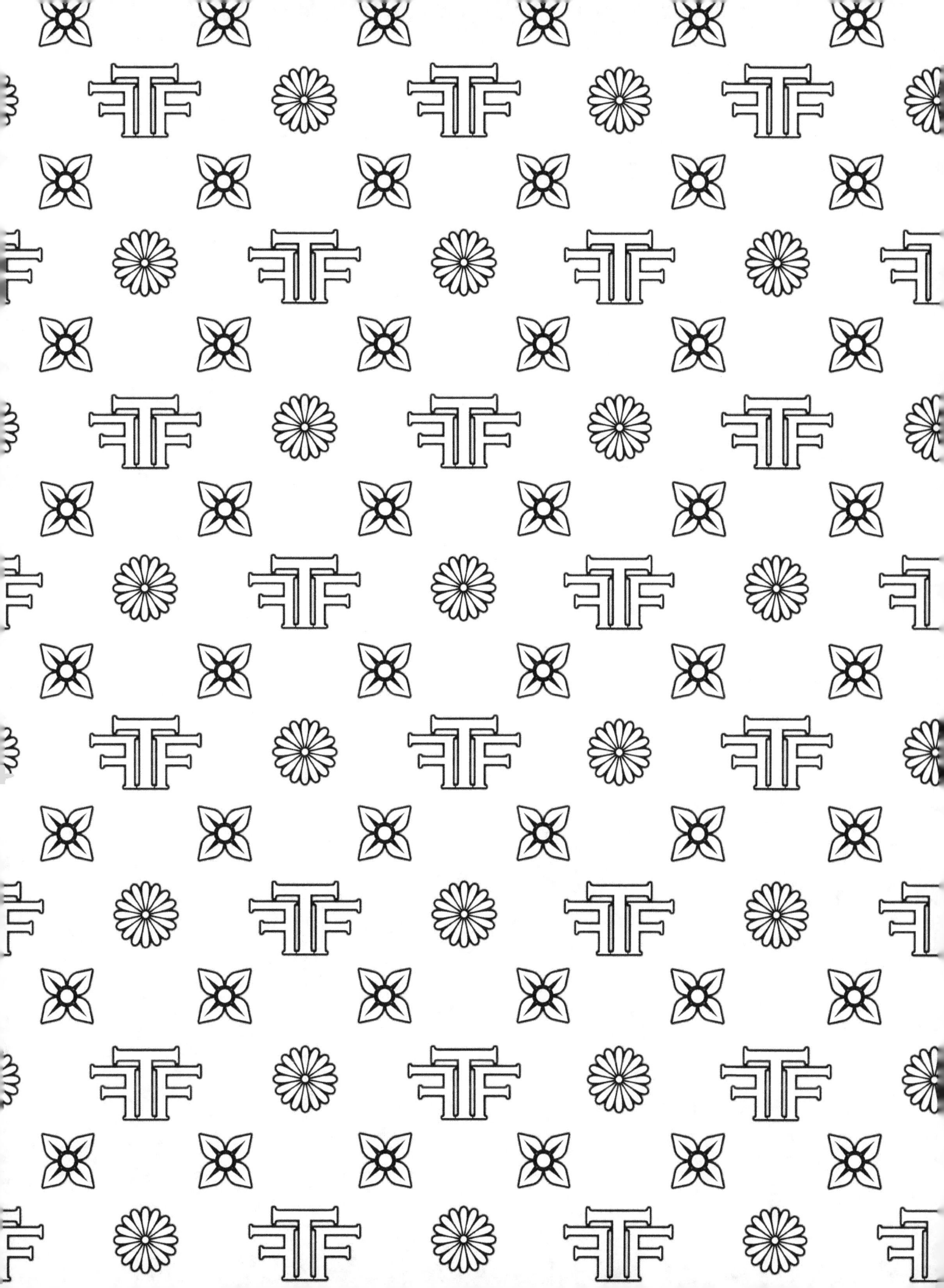

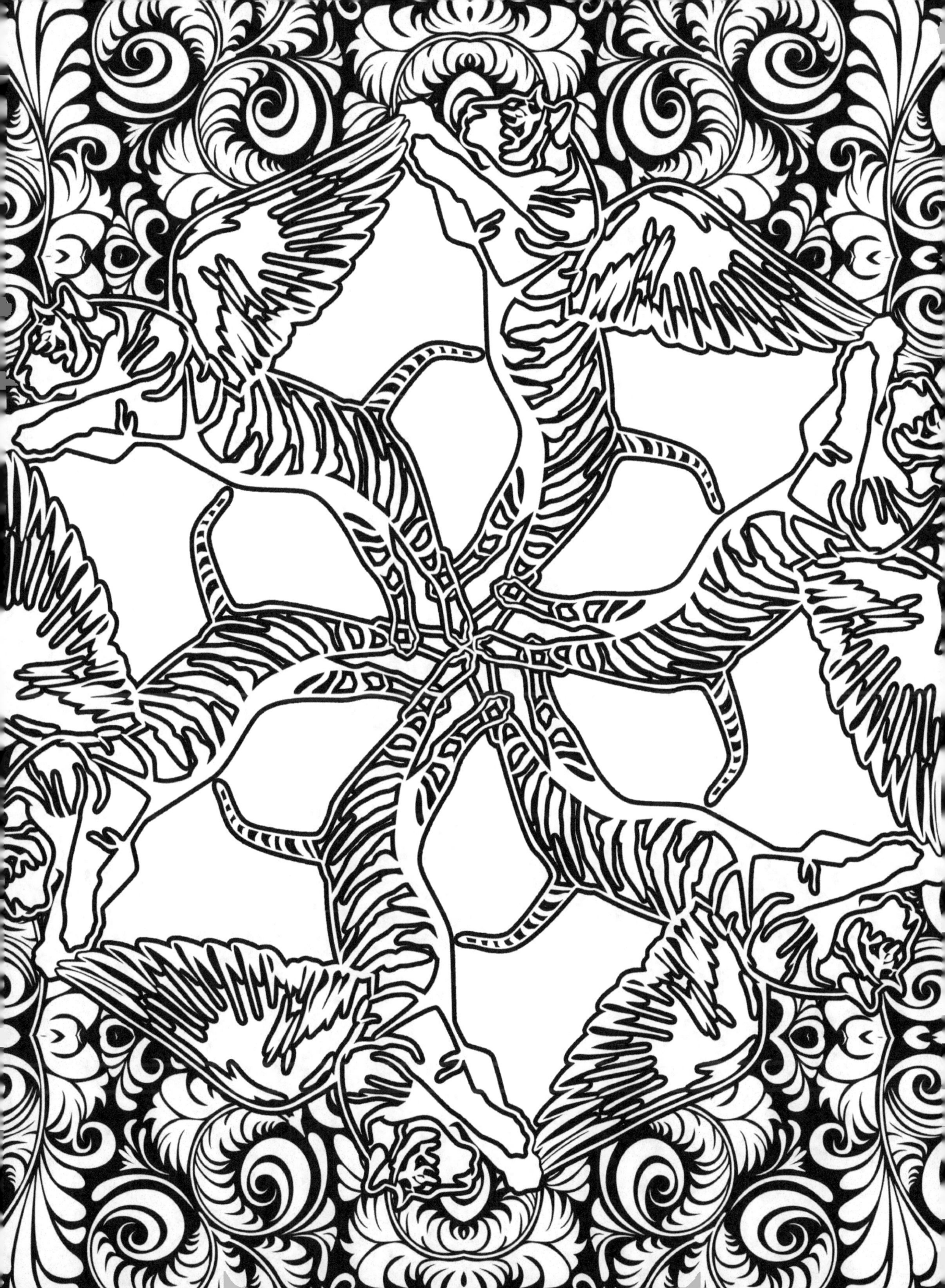

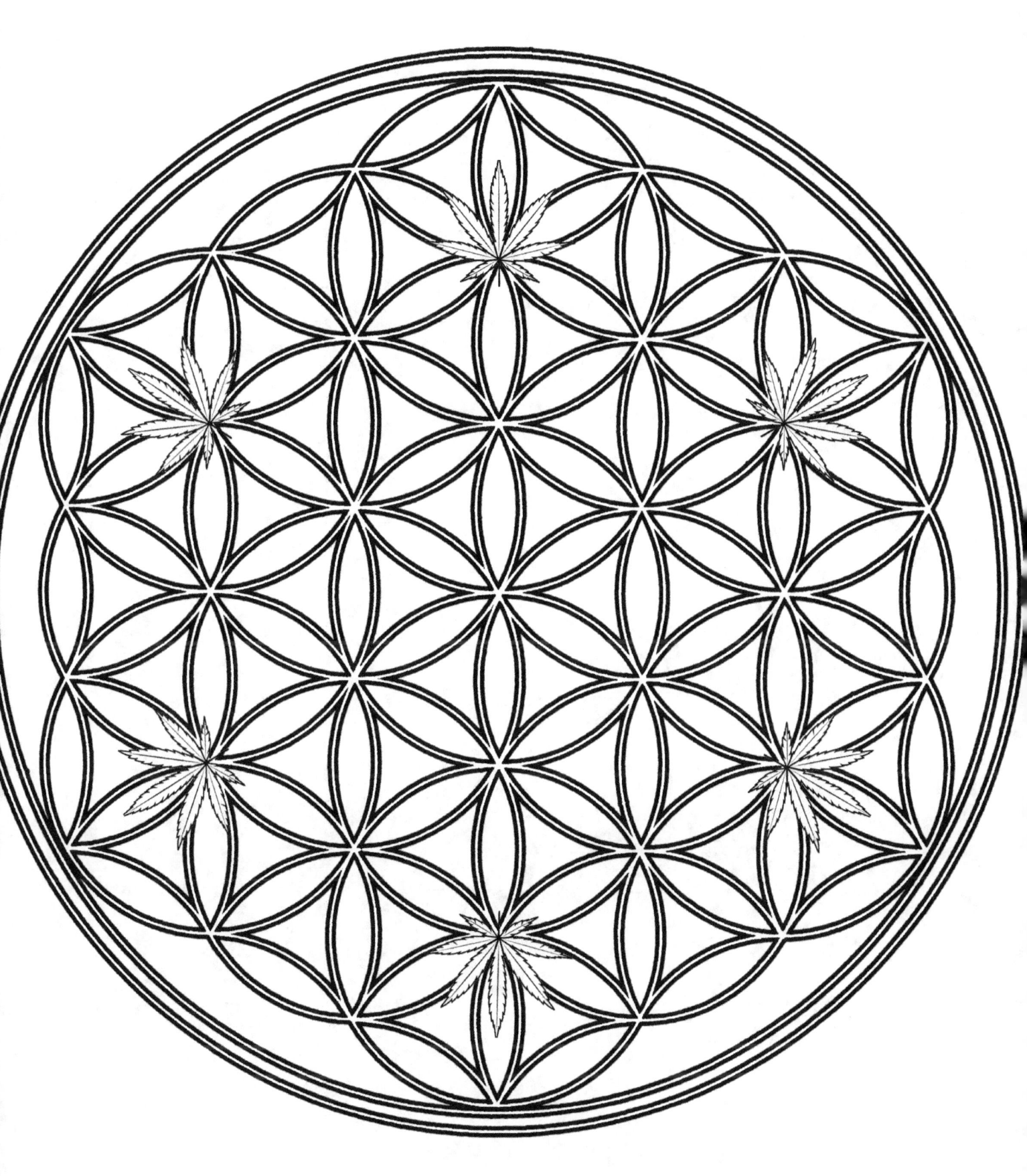

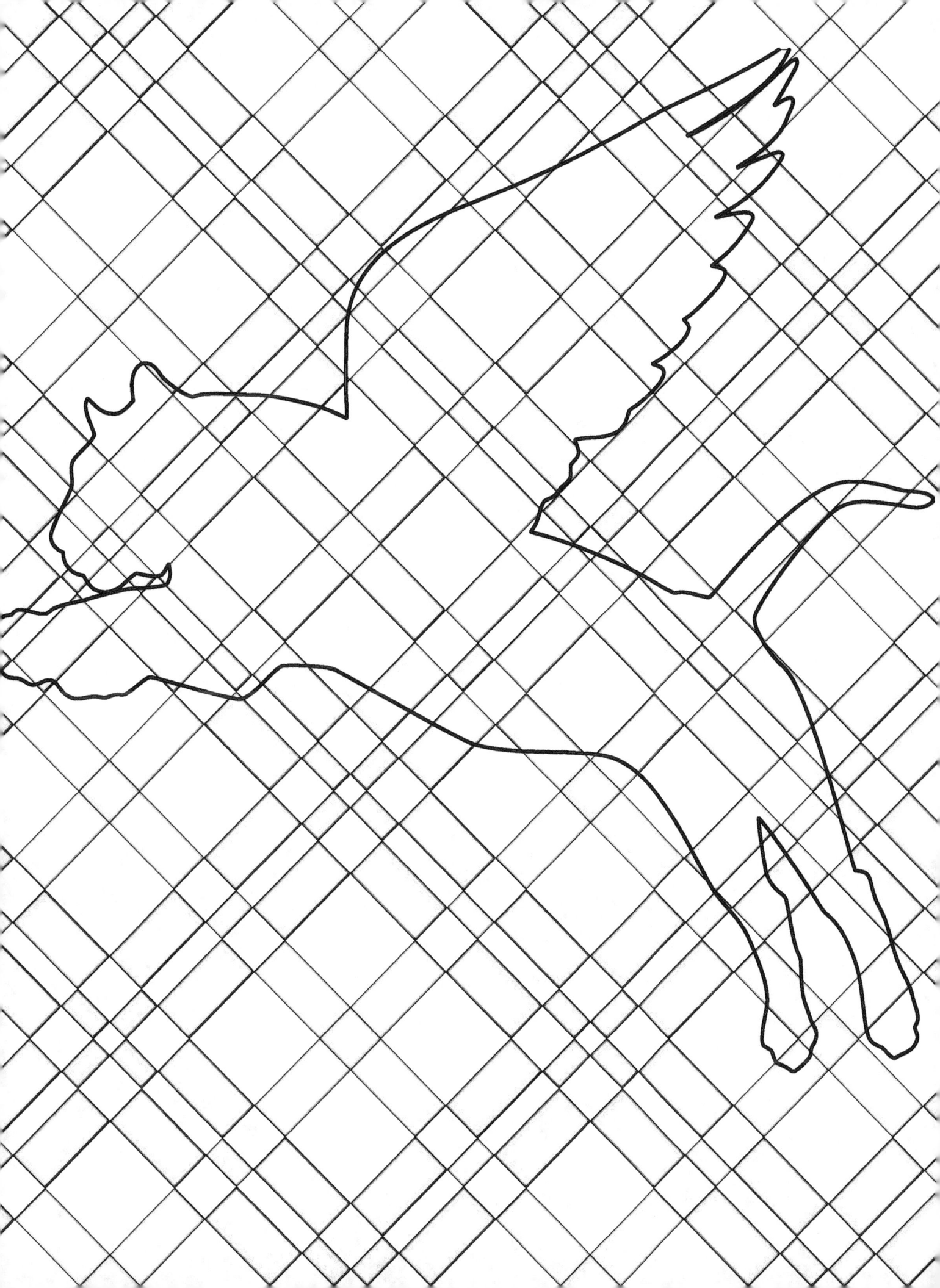

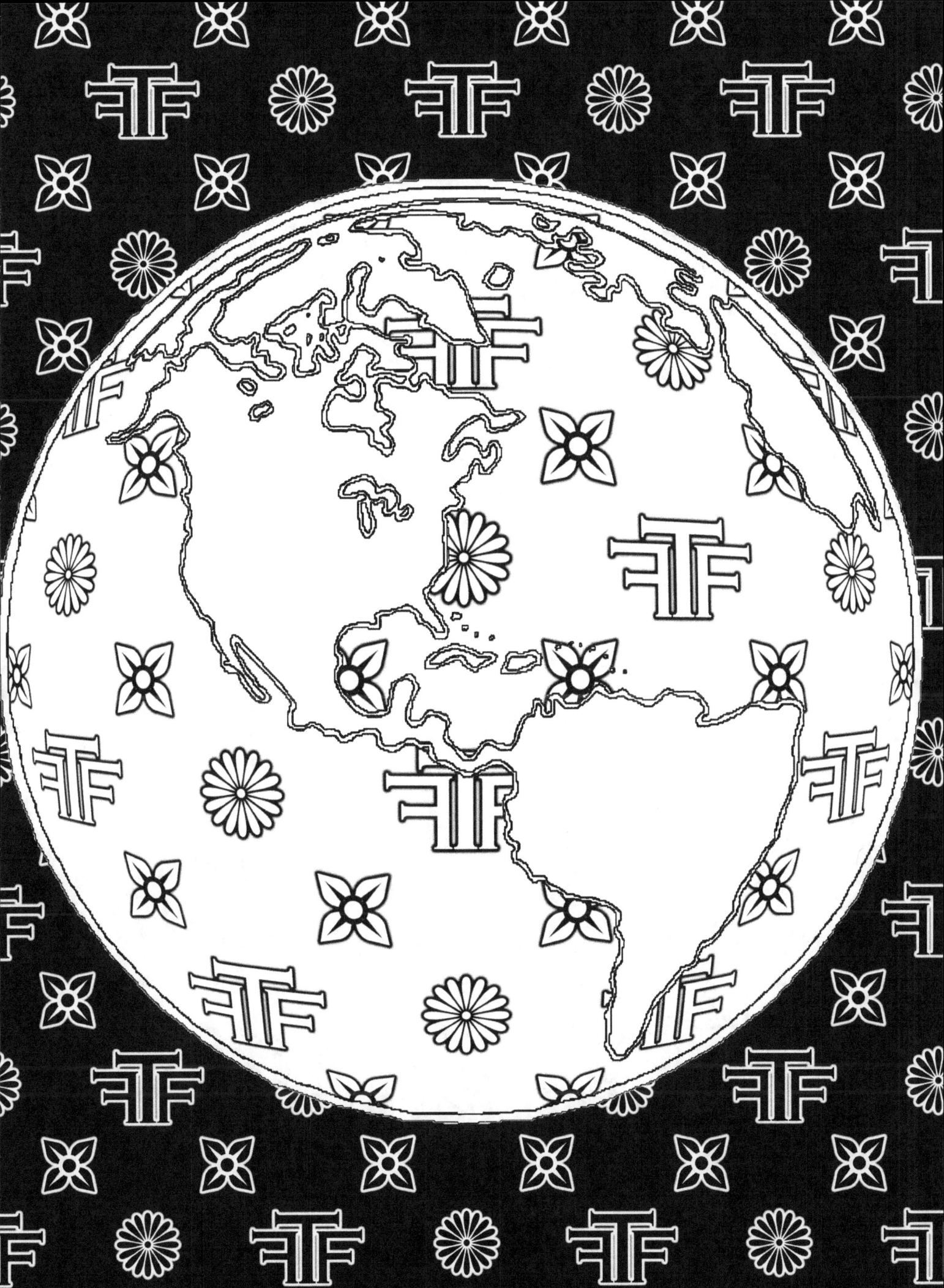

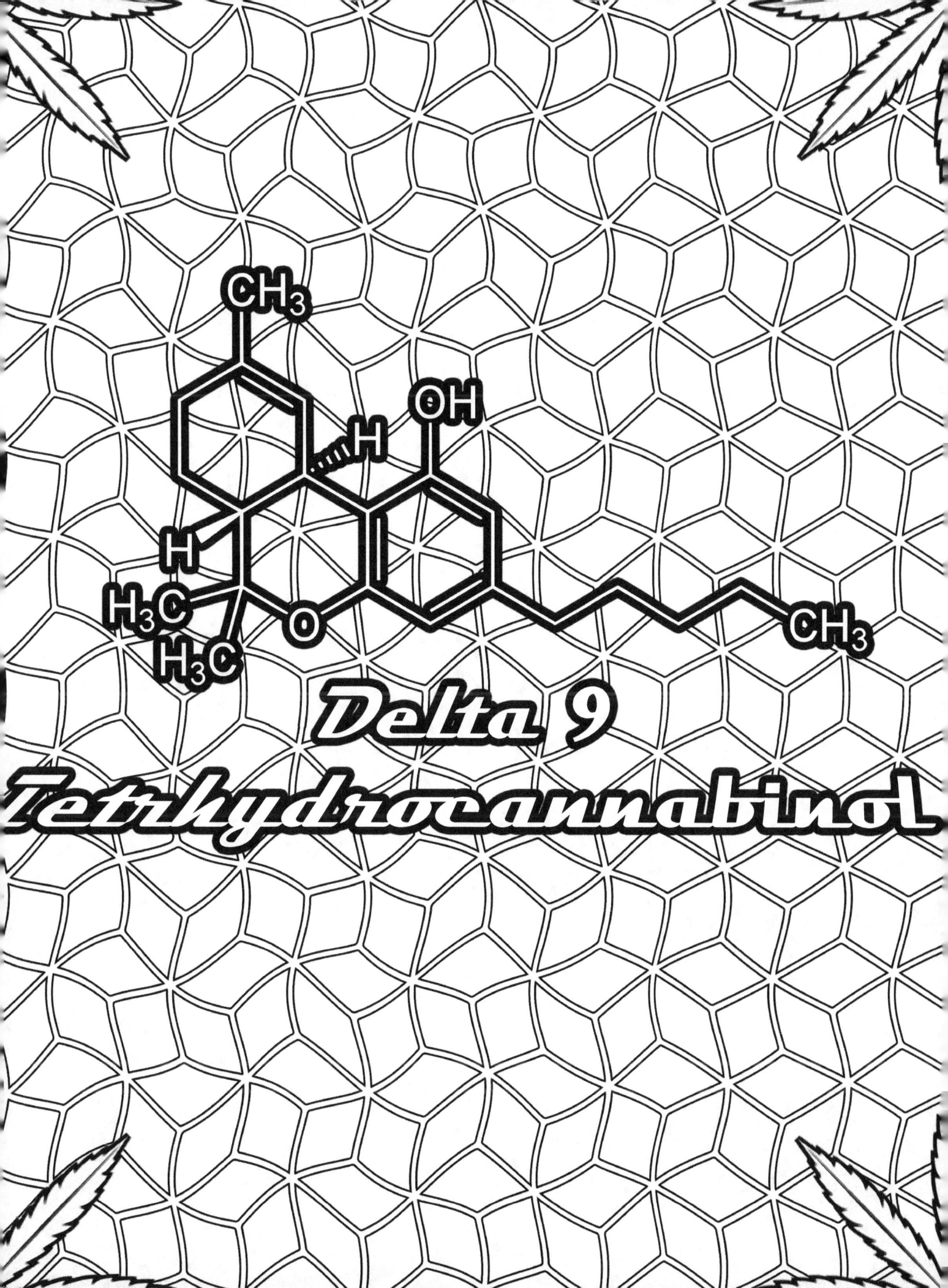

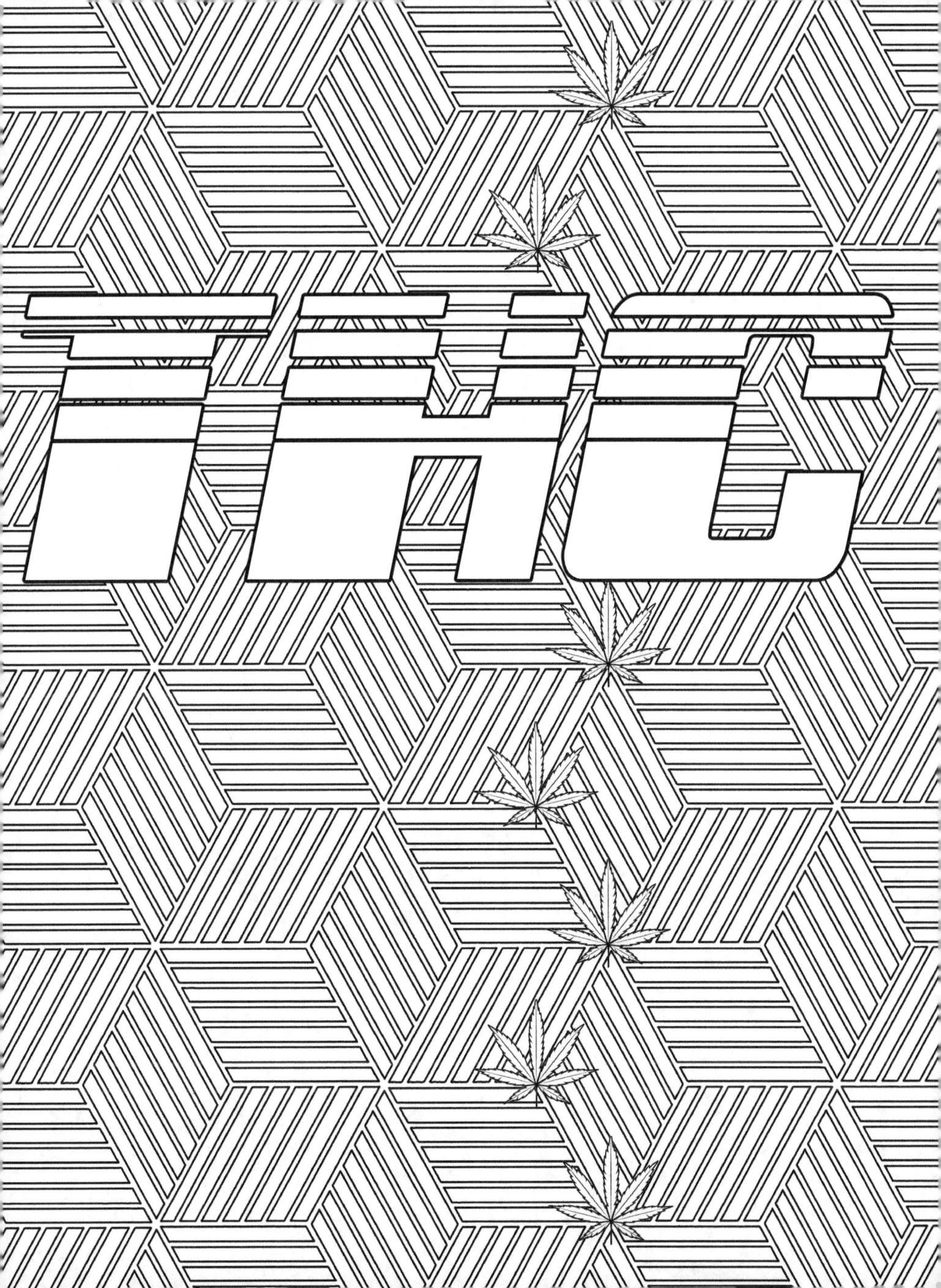

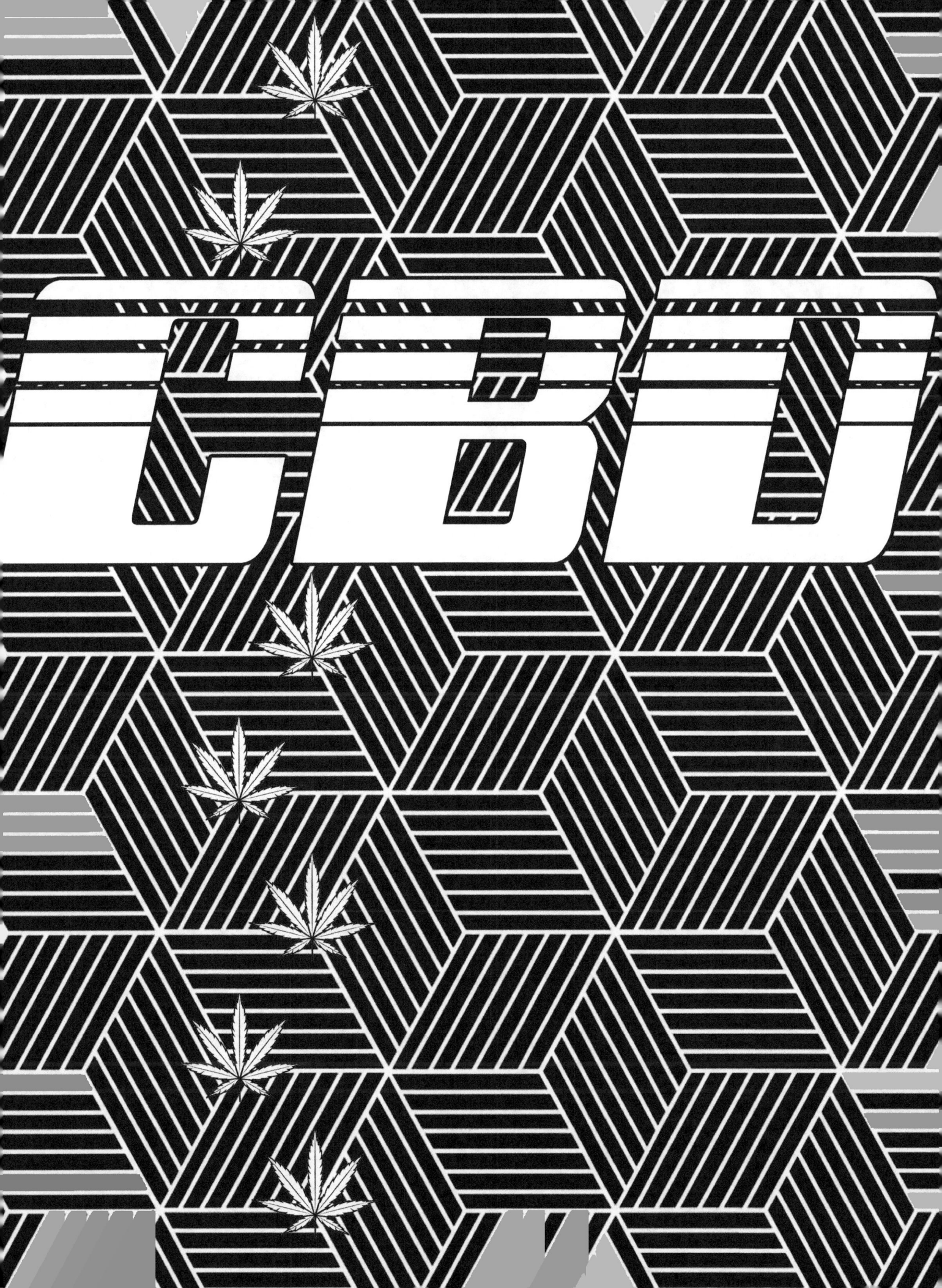

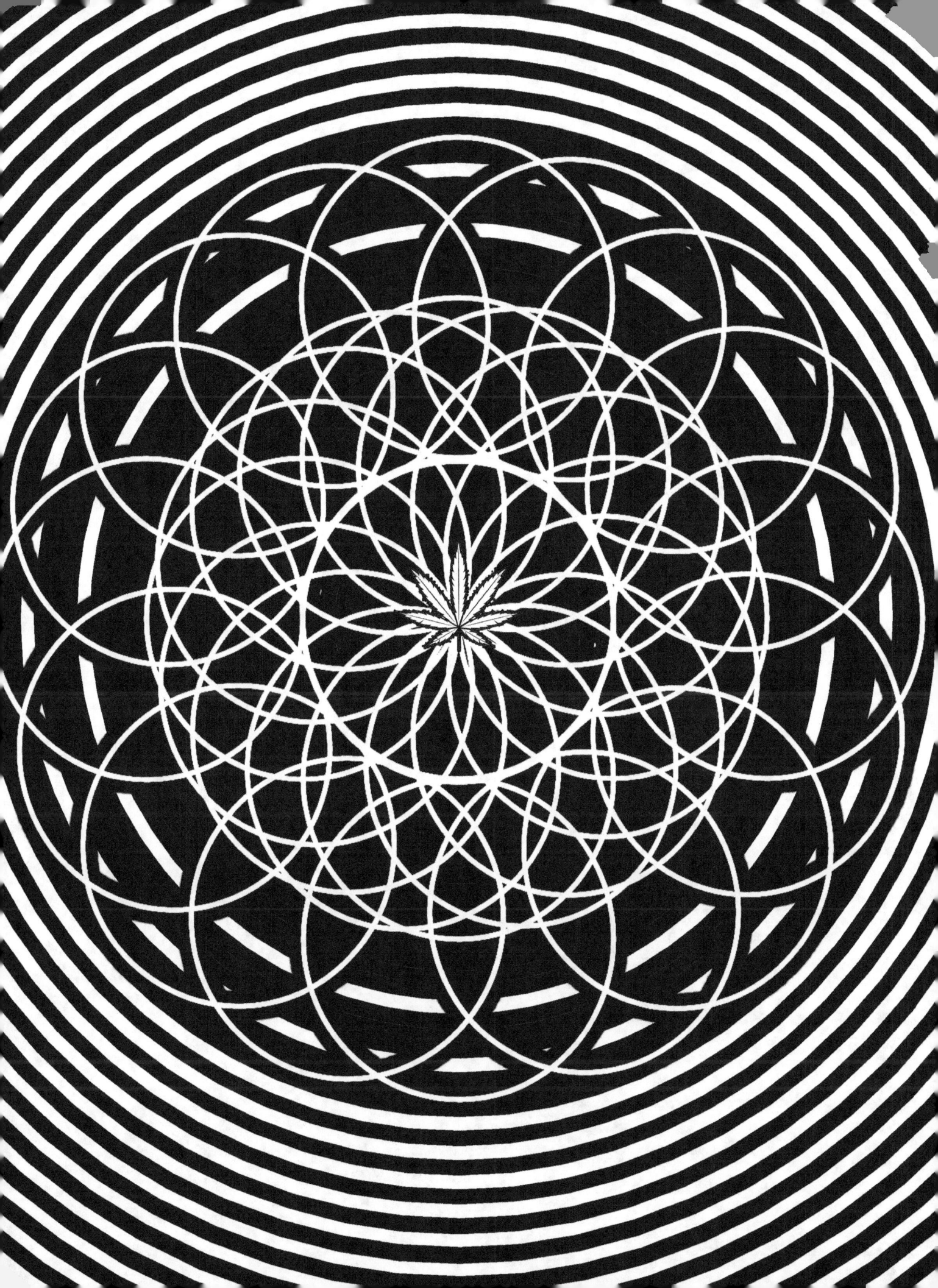

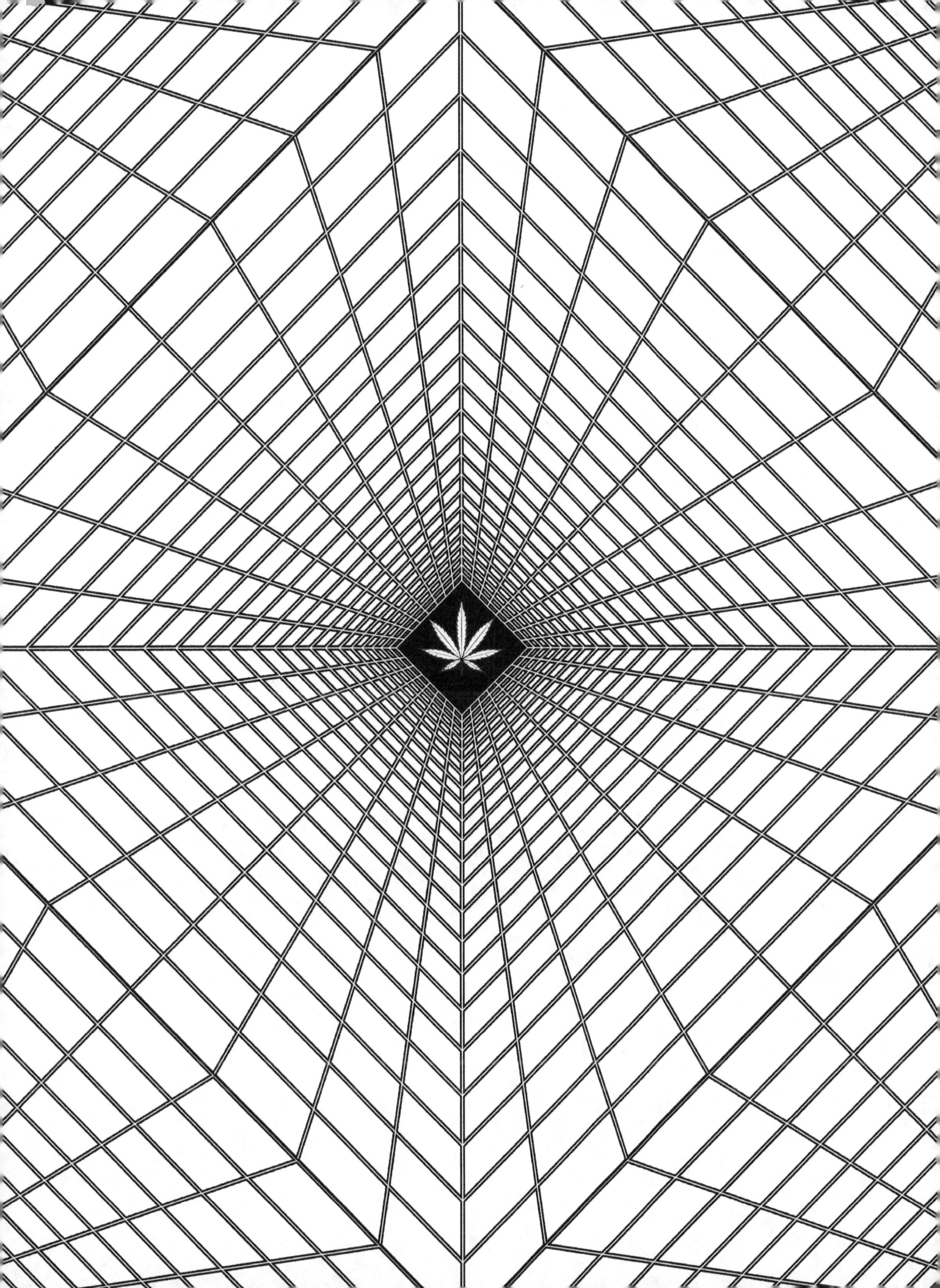

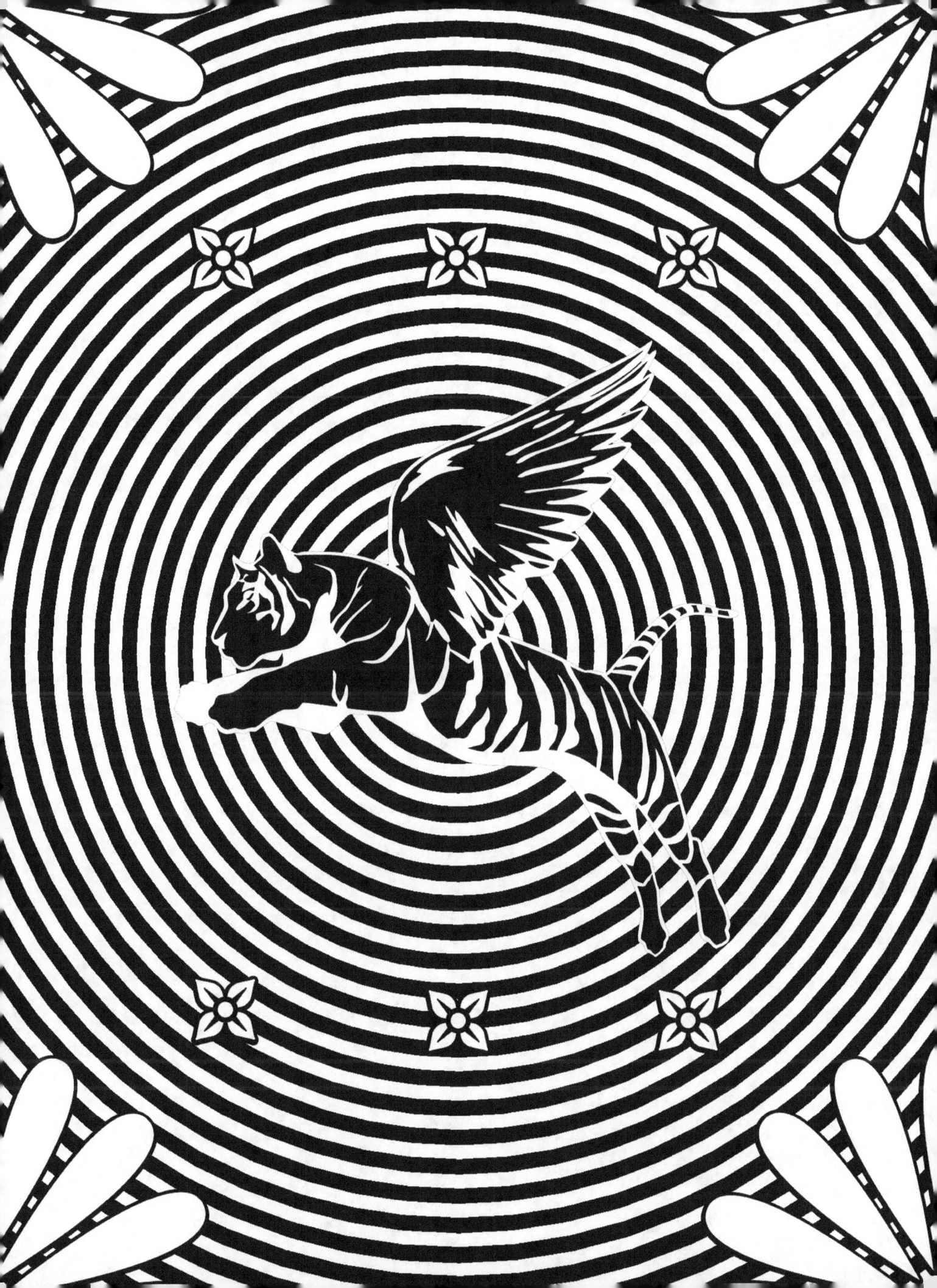

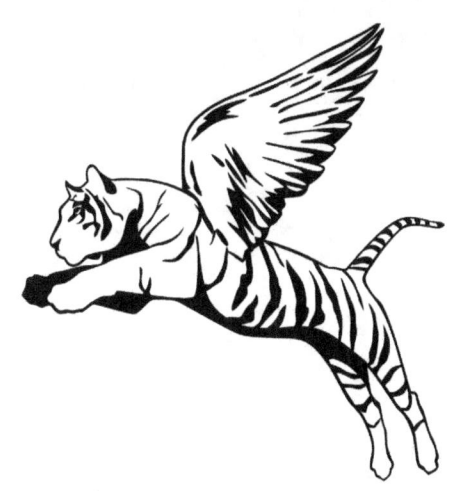

Flying Tiger Farm produces exquisite California cannabis on a sun drenched mountainside in the heart of Mendocino County. We are a solar powered, independent farm. Our sustainable farming methods encourage care for the soil, the groundwater, and the natural habitat. We emphasize producing cannabis that showcases distinctive varietal flavors and highlights the terroir of our unique region.

 ari@flyingtigerfarm.com

 @flyingtigerfarm

www.ingramcontent.com/pod-product-compliance
Lightning Source LLC
Chambersburg PA
CBHW082258220526
45469CB00009B/3062